Koala Joeys

Julie Murray

Abdo
BABY ANIMALS
Kids

abdopublishing.com

Published by Abdo Kids, a division of ABDO, PO Box 398166, Minneapolis, Minnesota 55439.
Copyright © 2018 by Abdo Consulting Group, Inc. International copyrights reserved in all countries.
No part of this book may be reproduced in any form without written permission from the publisher.

Printed in the United States of America, North Mankato, Minnesota.

052017

092017

Photo Credits: iStock, Minden Pictures, National Geographic Creative, Shutterstock,
©D. Parer & E. Parer-Cook p.7 / ardea.com

Production Contributors: Teddy Borth, Jennie Forsberg, Grace Hansen

Design Contributors: Christina Doffing, Candice Keimig, Dorothy Toth

Publisher's Cataloging in Publication Data

Names: Murray, Julie, 1969-, author.

Title: Koala joeys / by Julie Murray.

Description: Minneapolis, Minnesota : Abdo Kids, 2018 | Series: Baby animals |
    Includes bibliographical references and index.

Identifiers: LCCN 2016962295 | ISBN 9781532100048 (lib. bdg.) |
    ISBN 9781532100734 (ebook) | ISBN 9781532101281 (Read-to-me ebook)

Subjects: LCSH: Koala--Juvenile literature. | Koala--Infancy--Juvenile literature.

Classification: DDC 599.2--dc23

LC record available at http://lccn.loc.gov/2016962295

Table of Contents

Koala Joeys

A baby koala is a joey.

The joey is tiny when it is born.

It's the size of a jelly bean.

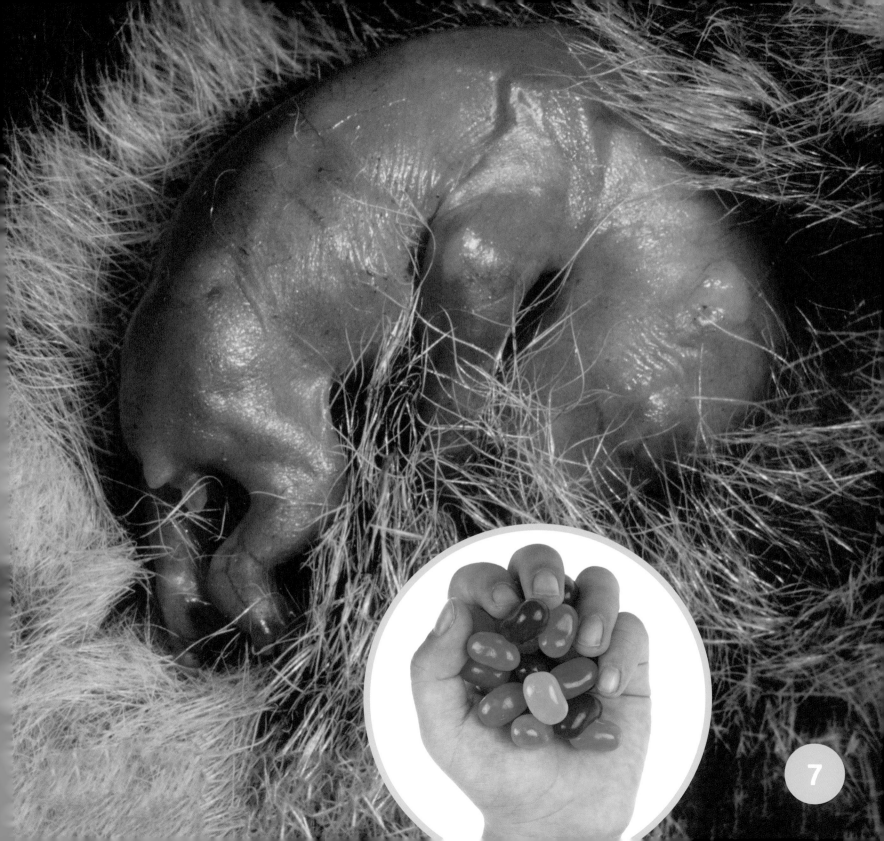

It is pink in color. It has no fur.

It can't see or hear.

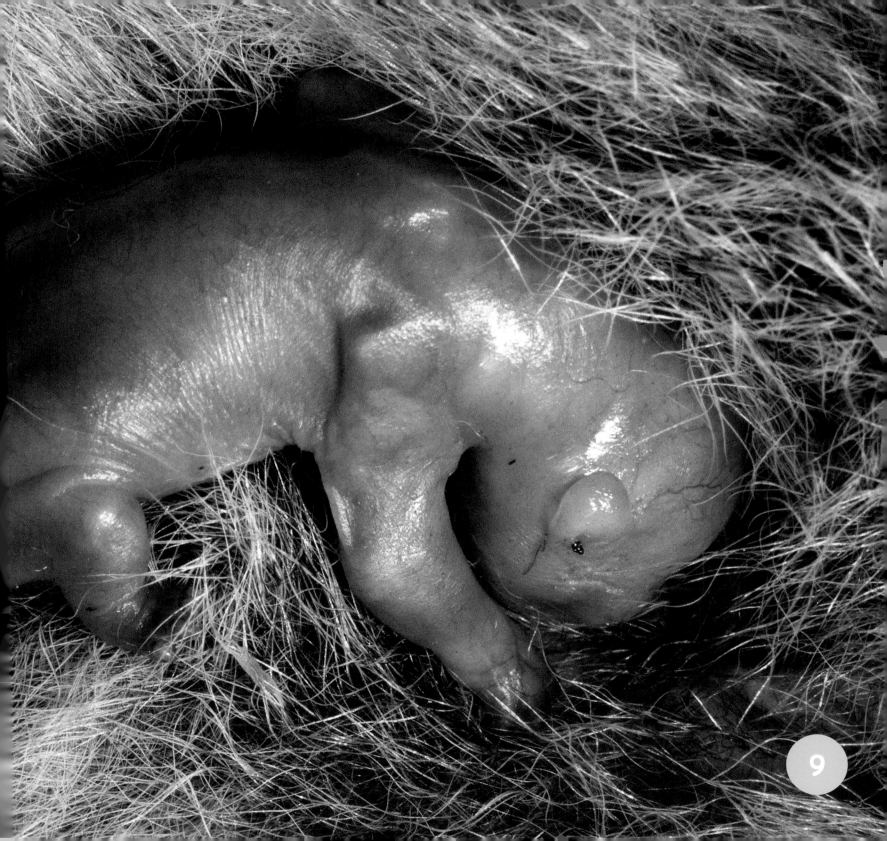

It is safe in its mother's pouch.

It stays there for six months.

The joey drinks its mother's milk. It grows.

Then it leaves the pouch.

It rides on its mother's back.

It grows **thick** fur. It is grey or brown in color. The fur keeps it dry.

It has long claws. These help it climb trees.

The joey eats leaves. Gum leaves are its favorite!

Watch a Koala Joey Grow!

newborn

7 months

2 years

3 years

Glossary

pouch
a stomach pocket where some animals carry their young.

thick
made up of a large number of things that are close together.

Index

abdokids.com

Use this code to log on to abdokids.com and access crafts, games, videos, and more!

Abdo Kids Code:
BKK0048